AMRAPALI

AMRAPALI

Archana Nayak

Translated by
Sanjeet Kumar Das

BLACK EAGLE BOOKS
Dublin, USA | Bhubaneswar, India

 Black Eagle Books
USA address:
7464 Wisdom Lane
Dublin, OH 43016

India address:
E/312, Trident Galaxy, Kalinga Nagar,
Bhubaneswar-751003, Odisha, India

E-mail: info@blackeaglebooks.org
Website: www.blackeaglebooks.org

First International Edition Published by
Black Eagle Books, 2024

AMRAPALI
by **Archana Nayak**

Translated by **Sanjeet Kumar Das**

Original Copyright © Archana Nayak
Translation Copyright © Sanjeet Kumar Das

All rights reserved. No part of this publication may be reproduced, stored in a retrieval system, or transmitted, in any form or by any means, electronic, mechanical, photocopying, recording or otherwise without the prior permission of the publisher.

Cover & Interior Design: Ezy's Publication

ISBN- 978-1-64560-562-1 (Paperback)
Library of Congress Control Number: 2024943481

Printed in the United States of America

Author's View

The Play *Amrapali* is based on a famous story of the Buddhist period in India. Generally, many stories and characters, as enshrined in the great epics of the Mahabharat and the Ramayan of India, are creatively transferred and have wider acceptability and readership among the public. The incidents of Buddhist and Jain texts scripted in Pali and Prakrit languages strongly impact contemporary life in society and literature.

While reviewing the literature of *Bauddha Bhikshunis* (female mendicants), I came across Ambapali, a Courtesan (Bride of the City) of Vaishali. There was a small state, Vaishali, in North India two thousand and six hundred years ago. It was the *Sangha*-governed Republic. A vast mango orchard was on the outskirts of this city. One day, while wandering, the mango grove's watchman was startled to see an abandoned newborn girl beneath a mango tree. As per the approval of the state council, the issueless watchman nourished and nurtured the girl. When he found the child under the mango tree, she was named after Amrapali/Ambapali/Amba.

Like a celestial nymph, Amrapali became a young nubile girl known for her beauty and charm. She was divinely graced. She was second to none in dancing and singing. Having participated in the Annual Dance

Programme, Ambapali was declared the 'Royal Court Dancer' by the State Republic. Because of her extraordinary beauty, the Merchants, the Barons, and the members of the State Council started fighting among themselves to be with her. So, the state Board of Council announced the Courtesan (Bride of the City) for the city's welfare. Every male in the town would have the right to spend time with her.

The anecdote of Amrapali's beauty and dance performance of sublime order had been spread worldwide. The insolent Emperor of Magadha, the enemy state of Vaishali Republic, Bimbisara, had disguised himself to enter the palace of Ambapali and received hospitality as a guest for seven days. When the State Council of Vaishali came to know about the matter, it immediately tried to arrest King Bimbisara; Ambapali helped him escape the spot. Then, the love story of Bimbisara and Amrapali was brought to the limelight. The State Council accused Ambapali of developing a love relationship with the King of the enemy state.

On the other side, the King of Magadha Bimbisara fought with the Vaishali Republic to marry Ambapali and won the state. However, Ambapali showed hesitation in moving to Magadha and leaving Vaishali. At this time, the most compassionate Lord Buddha reached the city. Ambapali surrendered at the feet of Tathagata Buddha and started to lead the life of a female mendicant with the hope of getting nirvana (Salvation).

I had determined to write a play on this topic. When I was talking to the young promising play director and the renowned film director Mr Himanshu (Chandi) Parija one day, he said to me, "I have been tired of directing plays on social issues for years. You write a play for me wherein there will be a good story, dance, song and the royal family backdrop." Suddenly, the story of Ambapali clicked in my mind, and I became active in penning down the story. He earnestly showed his interest in my story. I concentrated on the theme, and the result was what we see today.

I finished the play. After I handed over it to Himanshu Babu, I became confident. I was sure that I didn't have to do anything more about it. Then I realized he would not be interested in this high-budgeted stage show. But, within a month, I got an invitation letter to watch the play and was astonished. The play was first staged on 12 September 1988 at the *Kalavikash Kendra* by the 'Samabesha' Play Institute Tulasipur with the help of famous artists of Film Industry and Stage Artists very lavishly.

That day in the evening, it was raining cats and dogs. But the theatre lovers, despite the rainstorm, reached the Theatre Hall. The theatre was fully occupied. The audience's reaction made me realize that the play won the public's hearts.

This play was again staged with the direction of Himanshu Babu consecutively for two days at the Shailabala Women's College, Cuttack. I can admit wholeheartedly the contribution of Mr. Himanshu Parija to the successful staging of the play.

Archana Nayak

Amrapali: A Critial Evaluation

One of the renowned writers of Odia literature, Archana Nayak's Odia play *Ambapali*, is herewith given an English rendition as *Amrapali*, based on the legend as available in Buddhist Scriptures written in Pali language. Amrapali/ Ambapali/Amba are used interchangeably in the text to revolve around the main protagonist, Ambapali. The play deals with love, sacrifice, and women as the means of negotiation (*Nagaravadhu*: 'courtesan' or 'bride of the city') and her complete surrender to the lotus feet of Lord Buddha, the enlightened one.

Magadha was controlled monarchically, although Vaishali, the ancient capital of the Vajji dynasty, was governed democratically. Subsequently, the word for government was utilized. Their government was known as the "Vajji Sangha" or "Vajji Gana Parishad"; a Gana-sangha comprised several kings the populace chose to rule concurrently. Located north of Magadha, Vajji was one of the populated states of Ancient India. Vajji was ruled by a group of rulers, unlike Magadha, which had one ruler at a time.

Ambapali, a celestial nymph, a heavenly beauty, was found at the very outset as a newborn baby in a mango grove and adopted by one of the guards working there. She was a foster child to Basumitra and his wife Sujata, with the consent of the State Council, Vaishali. She was extremely good at dancing and singing. Her enchanting beauty and charm made her famous among the Royal Courtiers, Merchants, Barons and the Public. Because of her, the civil war sprang up inside and outside the state. Then, the state council members declared her as the 'Courtesan' or 'Bride of the City' or 'Royal Court Dancer'. Every state citizen can be with her to spend some time at her convenience. In the ancient period, this type of tradition was kept alive in some parts of India.

Smitten with her beauty, the king of the neighbouring state, Magadha, Bimbisara, disguised himself to enter her palace at midnight. He stayed there for seven days as a guest. Love glued their hearts together. Their relationship got public after Bimbisara›s secret departure from Vaishali. Magadha was the enemy state of Vaishali. King Bimbisara wanted to own Ambapali and make her the Principal Queen. Being inclined towards Buddhism, Amba denied the king›s proposal. She invited Lord Buddha to her palace for a feast and consecrated herself to Buddhism. Finally, she donated her mango grove (Ambapali Vana), where Buddha preached *the Ambapalika Sutra*.

Hindu philosophy is based on two essential aspects of human life: firstly, one comes to this world repeatedly to lead life birth after birth; secondly, one has to sever the relationship with the ethereal world and transcend the cycle of birth and death to attain nirvana (salvation). Buddhist ideology favours the second one. At the end of the play, Ambapali surrenders everything of her life at the feet of Gautam Buddha and joins his *Sangha* as a female mendicant. Amba realizes in the presence of Lord Tathagata, "Life on earth is temporary and meaningless. The body will be affected by old age, diseased and finally decayed on earth accepting death."

From a feminist point of view, this play can be discussed. Here, the protagonist Ambapali is declared 'the Bride of the City' or 'Courtesan' to be used as public property, as if she were an object. Her interest has been relegated to the background, keeping the state's welfare in view. Her love interest has been thwarted twice, initially for Soma, the erstwhile lover of her early youth and later for King Bimbisara, because of social stereotypes and criticisms. She has been made the courtesan against her strong opposition. Her voice is subdued and subsided against the social system.

Ambapali has sacrificed her love and life from the first to the last. From the very outset, she was discovered at the mango grove. She was unaware of her parents. She grew up with the love, care, and blessings of her foster father and mother. For her extraordinary beauty, the state council Vaishali declared her the 'Courtesan'. Her love for Soma withered subsequently. Her passion for King Bimbisara was also not paid attention to because she couldn't be a traitor for standing against her own state in her interest in the king of the enemy state. Then, she became mature enough to understand the philosophy of life and at last surrendered to Lord Buddha.

The theme of the original Odia text has appealed to me. I translated the Odia text *Ambapali* from Odia into English for global readership.

I have tried my best to keep the language as lucid as possible. While following the rules of equivalence and the rules of fidelity between the Odia language and the English language, I came across some natural shifts. The culture-specific terms of the source language texts are maintained as they are. Some deictic expressions of the Odia language are marked in the target language while translating.

I deeply revere Dr Archana Nayak for believing me to translate her text carefully. I convey my heartfelt gratitude to Sri Satya Pattanaik, the director of Black Eagle Books, U.S.A. and Sri Ashok Parida of the publishing house for their kind consent to publish the texts in time.

Sanjeet Kumar Das

DRAMATIC PERSONAE

Female Characters

Ambapali	:	Courtesan of Vaishali
Madhavi	:	Amrapali's Friend
Chitra	:	Amrapali's Friend
Sujata	:	Amrapali's Mother
Chapala	:	Amrapali's Attendant

Male Characters

Basumitra	:	Ambapali's Father
Bimbisara	:	Emperor of Magadha
Mahamantri	:	Chief Minister of Magadha
General	:	Head of Magadha's Army
Ganadhar	:	Vaishali's Chief Administrator
Sheelabhadra	:	One of the Councillors
General	:	Vaishali
Buddha	:	Lord Buddha, The enlightened one
Prabhakar	:	Nrutya Guru (Dance Teacher)
Soma	:	Ambapali's Fiancée

Councillor-I
Councillor-II
Councillor-III
Malunkaputta : A disciple of Lord Buddha
Buddhist Monk-I
Buddhist Monk -II
Buddhist Monk -III
Buddhist Monk -IV
Sentry

ACT-I

Scene-I

[After the curtain gets raised, a mango grove is seen. The watchman Basumitra wanders there at the dawn before sunrise. The cry of a newborn child suddenly echoes in the surroundings. Shocked, Basumitra stands up. Looking here and there, he runs to the root of a mango tree and finds a child...he picks up the newborn girl, abandoned there and clasping her anxiously; he earnestly conveys his gratefulness to the Almighty. O, Most compassionate Lord! I praise your greatness! You have heard my prayer after a long time. I have prayed before you, frequently beating my head at your feet to relieve me from the scathing remarks of issueless life...today, you have taken away my sorrows, miseries and plights from me by a 'celestial damsel'. Please accept my gratitude and bless the child. I will go home quickly to pass the information on to Sujata and hand over this precious gift to her...her emptied lap will be filled in. (Thoughtfully) But, first of all, I have to get the Council's permission to maintain the child...yes, yes, I have to take the consent.]

Scene-II

[It's the principal Hall of the Council. The Chief Administrator Ganadhar and other councillors are sitting on their chairs.]

Basumitra	:	(Entering) I bow down to all the esteemed members of the Council.
Ganadhar	:	What happened, Basumitra. Is there any issue with the Mango Grove?
Basumitra	:	No, Sir. No problem at all.
Ganadhar	:	Then? Well, what have you held in your hand?
Basumitra	:	A girl child-
Councillors	:	Girl child? Whose?
Basumitra	:	That I don't know, sir. I was roaming in the mango grove early in the morning. Having heard the cry of the child, I started running to find the source of sound. I saw someone left the newborn child at the root of the tree. I searched for, but I didn't find anybody there.
Sheelabhadra	:	A great injustice! There should be an inquiry for the culprits. They should be punished.
Councillor-I	:	That will be taken care of later. Now, who will look after the child?
Basumitra	:	Sir, I have come here to submit my plea before you for that. I am issueless. If I get permission from all the esteemed members here, I will nourish and nurture the child with utmost care.
Councillors	:	Thank you…thank you.
Ganadhar	:	Basumitra! Your plea is accepted and approved. You will look after the child.

	From today onwards, this child will be considered as your daughter.
Basumitra	: I am grateful to all of you. I have another submission before you all…today, at this moment, 'giving a name to my daughter', bless me and my child for the coming days.
Ganadhar	: Sheelabhadra Sir! Please, tell me a name.
Sheelabhadra	: (Thoughtfully) As the daughter is picked up from the mango grove, how would you feel if she were named after Ambapali?
Councillors	: Fantastic…fantastic name.
Basumitra	: (Paying respect to all) Please bless my daughter Ambapali. I promise to train her in all aspects. She will be an expert in writing poetry, dancing, and singing… She will be an extraordinary, second-to-none woman in the state.

[The stage light is off. The girl child grows into a teenager and, after that, an adult with the musical rhythm of instruments and the dance steps.]

Scene-III

[It's the mango grove. Ambapali and her two friends, Madhavi and Chitra, sit on a rock.]

Madhavi	: Amba, you have rested here longer than you have walked on the road. The evening is approaching. We have to go back a long distance.

Amba	:	Wait for a while, Madhavi. I am tired now. I feel pain in my feet.
Chitra	:	You have pain in your feet…but we don't feel anything.
Madhavi	:	What are you saying? Are our feet equal to her glowing and beautiful feet?
Chitra	:	Why? What's special about her feet?
Madhavi	:	We work hard daily like animals; our feet have come up with corn, while hundreds of crowns will be at her disposal.
Amba	:	No, Madhavi, don't say so.
Madhavi	:	I am not saying. The Saint Prajnananda has said so.
Amba	:	I am terrified.
Chitra	:	I mean to say what you are afraid of. Who gets a chance at that level? It's your fate.
Amba	:	It's not the opportunity. To me, it's a curse. Do you have any faith in the words of an ascetic?
Chitra	:	Amba, you see whether it is true or false. There is no need to think of it a lot. We have come to him playfully.
Amba	:	Yes, that was a jest for you. But I wanted to know about the darkness of my future.
Madhavi	:	Now that you have known…then, why are you unhappy? You will spend your life in the royal palace as the Queen. Hundreds of maidservants will be there to attend you.

Amba	:	I don't need all that. I will be happy with what an ordinary girl generally wants to get. I don't expect anything more.
Chitra	:	Listen to her! The elephant is ready to pour the water of the Golden pot upon her head, but she says she will go to the river with the pot to bring some water.
Amba	:	O,..you are making fun of me.
Chitra	:	I am not joking. Have I not denied you from the beginning that there is no need to know about the future? We will only visit the saint. You were excited to know about your future.
Amba	:	If his words hold good!
Madhavi	:	Let it be, what's the loss? Why are you so hesitant to be the Queen of a King?
Amba	:	Have you yet to hear what else he has told?
Chitra	:	What's that? We have yet to hear. Only you have listened to it.
Amba	:	The saint said, "Having received everything, you won't get anything. But what you will receive won't be received by anybody else."
Chitra	:	Stop talking nonsense. You are beating around the bush. No problem if you don't get anything. Let's return to our home.
Madhavi	:	(She helps Amba Get up.) It is really challenging to understand you.

	Sometimes, you murmur like the fountain, or at other times, you are silent like the clouds in the sky.
Amba	: Nothing like this.
Chitra	: Let's us roam here for a while. It's a scenic spot.
Amba	: No, it will be late. Evening sets in. we should go back.
	[A passerby enters.]
Stranger	: Can you please help me find some water? I am thirsty.
Chitra	: Can I know your name, please?
Stranger	: I am a wanderer. I need help finding my way. I am unaware of the place where I am now.
Madhavi	: This is the border region of Vaishali City.
Stranger	: How far is Magadha from here?
Chitra	: A small distance. Are you from Magadha?
Stranger	: No, I am a traveller.
Madhavi	: If you move in this direction to cover a small distance, you will see the brook. After taking water you come back. Someone may look after you. Instead, you return to the city. The night is approaching.
Pedestrian	: Thank you! I will do that. (Exit)
Amba	: We couldn't know his identity.
Madhavi	: He seems to be a prince.

Chitra	:	No, he is a spy.
Madhavi	:	(laughing) Why does the Council not appoint you as one of its members? You recognize having seen a stranger.
Chitra	:	(while thinking) He is not from Vaishali. However, he needs to find out where Magadha is. Other than these two states, there is no boundary between any other states. Then, where is he from?
Amba	:	Well, stop your guess or investigation. He may be of any other region, but he is very handsome.
Amba	:	Ok, Devi Amba eyes upon him.
Amba	:	No, no, I am not talking of his physique. He has a good personality.
Chitra	:	What?... Within a short period, his personality has pleased you. You would have worn him with a wedding garland if he had been here more.
Madhavi	:	Is she not of the age to make someone wear a wedding garland?
Amba	:	You are always joking! Let's return.
Chitra	:	No, let's wait for a while. He must be returning after drinking from the brook.
		If we accompany him, at least for this night, he will be a guest at your home. We can also know his identity.
Amba	:	I am going...You can accompany him and share your addresses as much as you want.

[Ambapali walks. Both of her friends follow her. The stage light is off.]

Scene-IV

[It's Ambapali's home. Her fostered father, Basumitra, and his nephew of a distant relationship, Soma, are engrossed in conversation.]

Basumitra	:	(Expressing disapproval) It's already evening. Why has Amba yet to return?
Soma	:	Why are you so much worried, Uncle? Amba has gone with others. Her friends have accompanied her. Because of some reason, they may be late.
Basumitra	:	You can't understand, Soma; if Amba is slightly late, I am worried. I am unsure why my mind dwindles with some ill omen. My heart gets perplexed if I don't see her for a moment.
Soma	:	How strange your affection is! One who doesn't know her won't believe that Amba is not your daughter.
Basumitra	:	No, no, don't say so, Soma. I and your aunt have worshipped God a lot for a child. We have sincerely prayed to the deities. Though we have not given birth to her, she is the blessing of the Almighty for us.
Soma	:	Whatever it may be, Uncle, God has heard your prayer.

Basumitra	:	You are true, my son. It seems that it happened yesterday. I am a watchman of the mango grove. I am happy and satisfied to stroll here and there from the morning to the evening. I still need to remember that auspicious day, but with the advent of the spring, each mango tree gets crowned like a king with its buds. The scent of the mango buds spreads in its surroundings in the storm. Like other days, I roamed the garden at the early dawn, before sunrise. When I took a turn, suddenly having heard the newborn baby's first cry, I saw a baby lying on a bed of leaves beneath a mango tree.
Soma	:	Was nobody seen at the nearby place? Did you wait for the child's mother or anyone to pick her up immediately?
Basumitra	:	Whom would I wait for? Can a mother throw her newborn baby like this at a distanced place?
Soma	:	Truly, Uncle. That woman must be cruel by heart. How could she give up her child?
Basumitra	:	Don't blame that woman; it's that man's fault. The father of this child must be more dangerous than her mother. Giving the assurance of marriage to the unmarried girl, he must have developed an illicit affair with her and later deserted her like a thief. You know our society; what could

		an unfortunate girl do at that critical moment? Sometimes, I get overwhelmed by that unlucky woman, my son.
Soma	:	Do you have any sympathy for that characterless lady? Had I known her, I would have killed.
Basumitra	:	No, Soma; don't say so. Without begetting Amba, if I am so overwhelmed, I can imagine the state of the mother who gave birth to Amba . No, no, we can't understand her. Being afraid of the society, she might have hidden her identity. But her mind must be searching for her daughter without our cognizance.
Soma	:	You are a very kind-hearted person, Uncle. It's shocking how well you have adopted an illegitimate child. Well, do others know about the 'tale of her birth'?
Basumitra	:	Yes, all know the story. I brought it to the notice of the Council and requested its members to hand over the child's responsibility to me. They considered my case, approved my plea, and named the child Ambapali, as she was found under a mango tree. Affectionately, I call her Amba.

[Amba's mother, Basumati's wife Sujata, enters.]

| Sujata | : | Can Amba's sorrows go if you repeatedly call 'Amba', 'Amba'? Now she is grown up. Having seen a suitable candidate, you should think of her marriage. You always |

	pamper your girl. You believe that she will always be with you. Well, son, you have been here so long. Meanwhile, you say how much he has uttered about her daughter. There is nothing else in the world.
Basumitra	: How do you know that I don't think of her marriage?
Sujata	: Had it been so, there would have been at least one marriage proposal. Alright, you do what you want. Where has she been so long? Please inquire into the situation. Why are you sitting idly at home? I am going to wave a light before the deity.

[Exit]

| Basumitra | : You say, how can I make Amba's mother understand? Our daughter is the repository of all good qualities. She is well-versed in dancing, singing, and reciting poems. But who will accept her as daughter-in-law since we don't have any information about her real parents, her caste and religion? Your aunt doesn't understand this. |

[Amba enters.]

Amba	: Baba! Baba!! (She becomes bashful seeing the guest.)
Basumitra	: Why were you so late, my child?
Amba	: No, Baba, we have all visited the saint Prajnananda's *ashram* for a while today. (She looks at the guest.)

Basumitra	:	Well, alright! You have never seen him earlier. He is Soma, my nephew who is distantly related to me. After you left the place, he reached our home. OK, you go inside, your mother was worried.

[Amba says 'Pranam' to Soma and leaves.]

Soma	:	(Soliloquy) This is Ambapali. An idol of beauty! A lack of bridegrooms for such a damsel! The person who will own her will be lucky.
Basumitra	:	What are you thinking, my son?
Soma	:	No, Uncle, nothing else.
Basumitra	:	OK, you rest here. Let me visit the mango grove.
Soma	:	No, Uncle. I don't need any rest. Let's move together. I will also see that mango tree from where you got your daughter.
Basumitra	:	OK, are you also thinking of that? Then, please, come with me.

Scene-V

[Being overwhelmed, Soma plays the flute under a tree in the mango grove. Ambapali enters. She earnestly listens to the flute sound. Soma sees Amba standing there suddenly and stops his flute.]

Amba	:	(Hiding her feelings) Baba, where are you?
Soma	:	Uncle has returned home a few minutes earlier.

Amba	:	I have yet to see him on my way.
Soma	:	He must have taken a rest somewhere.
Amba	:	Then, I am leaving. I came here to look for my father. (While departing) you are playing the flutes well. Some other day, I will hear.
Soma	:	You hear me now, Amba. I have to say something to you.
Amba	:	(Returning) To me! What?
Soma	:	It has already been one month I am staying at your home. When I wanted to return home, my Uncle denied me. He says, "I am over-aged now. It won't be possible for me to watch the mango grove. Again, you don't have anyone in your home. So better you stay here with us."
Amba	:	Don't you have anybody?
Soma	:	No, I don't have anybody now. In my childhood days, my father died, and I have not seen him. Last year, my mother breathed her last for the heavenly abode. Before my mother died, she told me this Uncle's name. That's why I came here to meet him. Now, he doesn't want me to leave this place.
Amba	:	Did you want to say this to me?
Soma	:	No, I wanted to know your opinions regarding this.
Amba	:	Me! What should I say?

Soma	:	Will I stay or not?
Amba	:	(Smiling) Your decision will be based on what I 'say'.
Soma	:	Yes, Amba.
Amba	:	Why?
Soma	:	The reason is straightforward: I have to stay at your home. How can I stay at your home without knowing your likes or dislikes?
Amba	:	My views don't matter. My father's decision is final.
Soma	:	Your father says, 'He will be lonely after you get married.' So,...
Amba	:	My marriage? No, no. I won't go anywhere. I will stay with my father.
Soma	:	Do the daughters always stay with their parents?
Amba	:	But, my marriage is not possible.
Soma	:	Why not possible?
Amba	:	Perhaps you don't know the story of my life.
Soma	:	I know that...I have heard about you.
Amba	:	After knowing all the details about me too...
Soma	:	Yes, but having seen a newly blown beautiful lotus, nobody thinks of its source 'clay'...having worn the necklace of pearls, no one searches for

	the meaningless shells…at the time of receiving the raindrops from the sky, no one thinks of its transformation of the saline water of any sea…who searches for the black spots in the moon in the full moon day? Like that full moon, you are as holy and virgin as the pearl. Your birth identity…(Having seen Amba crying)… why are you crying? Have I misbehaved with you? Pardon me, please.
Amba :	(While crying) You have not done anything. You know how my parents have nurtured me so affectionately. They have trained me well in learning, dancing and singing, but since the moment I knew the story of my life, I have been emotionally hurt. My mind gets clouded with untold plight. I am still determining who my parents are! Despite all my talents, I am an illegitimate child to the society. My life is meaningless.
Soma :	No, Amba. Don't think like that. Man does not have any right over birth; man can't fathom the mystery of the invisible God who allows someone to take birth at any place. So, it would help if you did not blame yourself for your birth.
Amba :	But not all people think like you. I am not the cause of my birth, but for that, I get insulted. I can understand, like other girls in Vaishali, I don't get the same respect in the society.

Soma	:	Amba, you are very conscious of yourself. For that, only your mind is always overpowered with languor and declines. Forget all that.
Amba	:	Will I forget? How can I forget that I am an illegitimate child? This question will remain a mystery forever…? Can't I ever know who my parents are?
Soma	:	No need to be emotional unnecessarily; don't dishearten yourself. Your foster parents have nurtured and loved you more than their own child. They haven't deprived you of anything. Is the blood relationship everything? Don't you give importance to their love and affection?
Amba	:	It means a lot to me. My heart always bows before them with gratefulness. But I can't claim my rights before them like other girls.
Soma	:	Oh, I see! You want to claim your rights over somebody.
Amba	:	No, no. You mean it differently.
Soma	:	No, why? Yes, please, Amba. The person you want will be happy.
Amba	:	But, no one will accept me as the wife.
Soma	:	If anybody agrees, will you say 'yes' to him?
Amba	:	(Astonishingly) What do you want to say?
Soma	:	If you don't have any objection, I am ready to accept you as my wife. (Eagerly, looking

	at Amba's face) say, Amba, please. If you agree, I will tell my Uncle. Otherwise, I will return to my village today. I can only stay here for a short time.
Amba	: Why not?
Soma	: How will I make you understand this? I have heard that the fostered daughter of my distantly related Uncle Basumitra is very beautiful. I have been interested to see her at least once. Having reached here, my wish to see her is getting converted to marry her. I am very excited and inclined towards you. If you don't agree to this proposal, I…
Amba	: (Bashfully) Please, you can talk to my father regarding this.
Soma	: (Happily) Is it 'yes', Amba? Do you agree with my proposal? Then, I will be the most fortunate guy in this world.

[Madhavi calls Amba from a distance? They try to come to their normal position. Madhavi enters.]

Madhavi	: Amba! (Seeing Soma, she stops there.)
Amba	: Madhavi, come here. He is…
Madhavi	: He is your father's distantly related nephew.
Soma	: Well, Amba, I see where my Uncle is. You come with your friend. (He leaves.)
Madhavi	: Did you come here alone or with any friend?

Amba	:	Madhavi!
Madhavi	:	Speak me the truth. How far have you gone?
Amba	:	He wants to marry me.
Madhavi	:	Is it so? You love each other secretly. But I am aware of it now.
Amba	:	I don't know whether I love him, but I want to marry him. That's why I have been here in this sorrowful state for a long time without any identity. I am the fostered child of someone; I am fatherless, motherless and without any brother and sister. If I get married, I will get my husband's identity. I am someone's wife. I will be identified as the wife of that person. Whether he is poor or rich, handsome or not, it doesn't matter to me. Then, we will go to a place leaving the state where nobody will try to know my past. There, I will be known as someone's wife and somebody's mother. I don't have any other expectations in life.
Madhavi	:	I know, Amba. Your 'story of your birth' runs after you like a shadow of an evil force. You must remember that. Your life is not peaceful at all. Then, Soma agrees to accept you as his wife. He is ready to marry you despite the social stigmas. Let your life be blissful, having received him as your husband.
Amba	:	Yes, Madhavi, the uncertainty of marriage

		that ruined my life and caused me unrest for a long time now is over.
Madhavi	:	Today, I will tell to Chitra and Nanda. They will be very happy to hear good news.
Amba	:	No, Madhavi, please keep it a secret now. Who knows what's happening next?
Madhavi	:	OK, I am bothered when you are apprehensive. Let's go to find our friends.

Scene-VI

[This is Ambapali's room. She looks outside. Madhavi enters.]

Madhavi	:	Amba, do you listen to the announcement made in our state? Where are you looking at? What happened? Why are you so absent-minded?
Amba	:	It's nothing.
Madhavi	:	It's nothing, which means there is something. Please tell me.
Amba	:	He assured me. He will come on the next full moon day.
Madhavi	:	Few days are left. Why are you so upset?
Amba	:	Not for that, Madhavi; But why I am so worried I can't understand.
Madhavi	:	Not that's the only reason you are worried for. Ah, my dear friend! You can't bear a day of separation.

Amba	:	That's not at all. I have the patience to wait for Soma for my entire life. But I doubt whether my fate can tolerate my happiness!
Madhavi	:	You always have unnecessary apprehensions. Leave that story. Do you know what I have come for?
Amba	:	What's that?
Madhavi	:	This morning, the drumbeater of the Council announced door to door that a dance competition would be organized at the Conference Hall of the Council on the eve of the 'Spring Festival'. The top dancers of the state will join the programme. You will certainly join. I have come here to tell you that.
Amba	:	No, Madhavi, I am not interested in that.
Madhavi	:	What do you say? What you have learnt with solid perseverance and dedication for many years can go in vain?
Amba	:	I am not interested in dancing in the Royal Court.
Chitra	:	(Entering) Why are you not showing your interest in dancing in that court? Who leaves this opportunity? How many well-trained dancers are here in the state? However, you are also gorgeous. You are going to win the award of the 'Best Dancer'.
Amba	:	I will think about it.

Chitra	:	What will you think? I would have gone alone, not informing you if I knew how to dance.
Madhavi	:	(Jokingly) Why can't you dance? Who has said this? But, once you start dancing, there is doubt whether the audience will watch or leave the spot, being afraid of the situation.
Chitra	:	Don't irritate me.
Madhavi	:	Who has come to irritate you?
Chitra	:	Were you acquainted with dancing? You would have said a lot.
Madhavi	:	Everybody knows that I don't know dancing. That's why I am saying Amba should not leave this opportunity. If no one watches the dance, what's the use of putting much effort into that? It's a golden opportunity to showcase your talent to the public.
Basumitra	:	(Entering) Yes, my daughter, It's your chance to prove your talent. The city's people will know and appreciate the skill of an ordinary watchman's daughter who has mastered the art of dance so well by her perseverance.
Amba	:	Baba (Daddy)!
Basumitra	:	Yes, my dear daughter. I don't have any recognition in the state. Nobody knows me. From childhood, I have trained you with an aspiration that you will be

		recognized in our land for your talent. I will be known as the father of Amba.
Amba	:	Yes, Baba, I will certainly participate in the competition.
Basumitra	:	I will inform your Guru Prabhakar Sharma. He will also be prepared for that day. (Exit)
Madhavi	:	There is no need of preparation for Guru and his disciple. Dancing and singing are their inborn talent. His blood corpuscles get excited at the anklets' musical rhythm and jingling sound. Ambapali is herself the 'Goddess of Dance'.
Amba	:	Stop praising me.
Chitra	:	If anybody would have praised me like this!
Madhavi	:	Do you know who will praise you? One who can't distinguish between the cuckoo's and the crow's voices will applaud your voice.
Chitra	:	Madhavi, I will beat you today.

[Chitra runs after Madhavi to get hold of her. Amba obstructs them. Meanwhile, Guru Prabhakar Sharma and Basumitra enter. Chitra, Madhavi and Ambapali show respect to Guru.]

Guru	:	God bless you! Well, Amba! Are you prepared for the show?
Madhavi	:	She has almost denied it, Guruji. Uncle and I have been able to convince her at last.

Guru	:	Why was she disinterested?
Basumitra	:	No, no, it's not that. She denied dancing in the *royal court*.
Guru	:	She is a child. She needs to be more mature to understand anything well. Perseverance only bears the result with the approval. It's the first chance of her life. Suppose she becomes successful in dancing before the King, the Council members, the intellectuals of the higher strata of society, well-trained artists, and the citizens of the high-class society; she will earn social prestige and get awards and laurels in her life.
Madhavi	:	Yes, Guruji, we have also made her understand the same.
Basumitra	:	Madhavi, go inside to tell your aunty that Guruji has come. [Madhavi leaves.]

Please, have your seat.

[Guru Prabhakar Sharma sits in the place specified for and plays with the traditional musical instrument Mridanga earnestly. The resonant sound of music reverberates in the room. All are listening to it.]

ACT-II

Scene-I

[It's the Conference Hall of Vaishali state. The esteemed members of the Council sit on their specified chairs and are present the intellectuals and the Barons of Vaishali. The 'Dance Programme' is organized with pomp and grandeur. At the end of each dance performance, the Chief Councillor addresses one of the Council members, Sheelabhadra.]

Ganadhar : Sheelabhadra, Sir, I would like to thank you for organizing this 'Dance Programme' on behalf of the Council. Young girls are so expert in dancing and singing. I am surprised.

Sheelabhadra : You will be mesmerized when you will watch Ambapali's dance.

Ganadhar : Ambapali? Who's she?

Sheelabhadra : Ambapalli is the daughter of a watchman working in the mango grove of Vaishali. She is a beautiful damsel who can defeat celestial dancers like Rambha and Urvashi in her art of dancing.

Ganadhar : Where is Ambapali?

[Ambapali enters dancing. Saying 'pranam' to all, she starts her *Bhubanmohan Kala* (the art of enchanting the world)... at the end, all the audience applauds, saying, "Marvellous, wonderful".]

Ganadhar : Great! Great!! Ambapali. We have been pleased having watched your dance performance. You are divinely blessed and second to none.

[Saying *pranam*, she stands up.]

Sheelabhadra : The esteemed members of the Council have watched all the performances. The programme comes to an end. Now I request the respected members to select the 'Best Dancer' for this evening.

All Members : (in Unison) There is no need for selection here. We all unanimously agree that Ambapali is the best dancer.

Ganadhar : Ambapali, you are the pride of Vaishali. I feel proud to award you as the 'Best Dancer'. Because of your extraordinary performance, Vaishali will be famous.

One Member : Let the Guru and father of Ambapali be invited to the Conference Hall of the Council. (Guru Prabhakar Sharma and Basumitra enter. Respecting Guru, he says.) Sir! The bright disciple of your teaching and training is Ambapali. We honour you with the highest 'The Gem of Dance' Award of the state for your excellence and exemplary perfection in the field of Arts, and a 'Dance Hall' will be built up for you on behalf of the state to train the young boys and girls in the coming days.

[Huge clapping]

Sheelabhadra : His Majesty is Ambapali's father, Basumitra.

Ganadhar : Basumitra, you are 'Great'! Being an ordinary watchman, you have made Ambapali a devout practitioner of dance performance since her childhood days, and the entire community of artists is grateful to you. On the eve of this occasion, I have sanctioned 'a fixed emolument' for you to receive from the state's 'Cultural Fund' every month. You will comfortably receive the amount until you breathe last. There is no need to watch the Mango Orchard.

All Members : Good decision!! (Clapping)

Scene-II

[This is Amba's home. Basumitra and his wife Sujata talk to each other.]

Basumitra : Sujata! My wishes are fulfilled after a long time. All the people of Vaishali now praise me. While walking on the road, they say, 'See, Ambapali's father is going. You told me earlier why I allowed her to be trained in dancing and singing. An extremely talented Girl like Amba will be found neither in this state nor in the adjoining ones.'

Sujata	:	You visited all the states…(laughing) How could you know that no one is like your daughter?
Basumitra	:	No one is there. No one will be like her. My daughter is the first and the last.
Sujata	:	I say, so much pride is not good.
Basumitra	:	This is not my pride; it's my glory. How can you understand? When we nurtured Amba in her childhood in love and affection, you forgot everything; I didn't think of her birth mystery. That's why I was determined to make her all-in-one so that people would look at her only, forgetting her birth history. She will be her own identity.
Sujata	:	That's right. Your wishes are fulfilled. Now you can think of our daughter's marriage.
Basumitra	:	I don't have to think about that. Soma is coming on the next full moon day. Then, we will finalize the 'Marriage Date'.
Sujata	:	I am not saying that. Nobody knew us earlier. Now, we are well-known and recognized. So you have to invite a lot of people.
Basumitra	:	Yes, yes, you are right, Amba's mother. Now, our situation is different. Don't worry about that. I have saved some good amount for Amba from the very beginning. We have to be conscious of those who

	will come after getting our invitation. Marriage expenditure is acceptable for us. Soma will stay with us.
Sujata	: Does he agree to stay here?
Basumitra	: I think he won't disagree with our proposal. I will spend my time with my grandchildren in this old age. I can't live without Amba.
Sujata	: Yes, you say that only. You can't stay leaving your daughter, but you are talking about the grandchildren.
Basumitra	: O, you are right. Well, where is Amba now?
Sujata	: She must have gone to meet Madhavi.

['Is Basumitra at home?' is heard outside.]

Basumitra	: Who's there? [A messenger enters.]
Messenger	: You and your daughter reach the Conference Hall of the Council as soon as possible.
Basumitra	: Why, sir?
Messenger	: I don't know. I must execute the order. I am leaving. You come soon. [Exit]
Sujata	: Is there anything wrong? Why does the Council call you again?
Basumitra	: You suspect everything. They may plan to give some awards to Amba. They have invited me to that.
Sujata	: No, no, there is something wrong. Amba, my child; God bless you.

Basumitra : Hello…call our daughter soon… otherwise, we will be late.

[Both of them stroll hurriedly from one side to the other.]

Scene-III

[It's the Conference Hall of Vaishali. All the Council Members are sitting. The Chief Councillor is thoughtful. The situation appears to be critical.]

Ganadhara : We have to take an important decision today for which all of you have been invited to this meeting. Some of you might guess what the reason can be. I am still helping you all understand. All of you can remember, a few days earlier, a 'Dance Programme' was organized here and many girls participated.

Sheelabhadra : The 'Best Dancer' award was given to Ambapali, the daughter of a watchman working in a mango orchard.

Ganadhar : Yes, today we have to decide on that, Ambapali.

Member-I : Decision about Ambapali? What's the matter?

Ganadhar : The art of perfection and excellence she showed in the dance that day is widely discussed in the neighbouring states. The messenger says the heads of the states, like Videha, Kalama and Malla, plan to invite Ambapali to their states. If we send

	Ambapali to their states accepting the invitation letters,...
Sheelabhadra :	Maybe they won't allow Amba to return to our state.
Member-II :	That may be their planning.
Ganadhar :	Then, we have to battle with them. Again, if we don't accept their invitation, we may endanger our diplomatic relationship with them. But the most dangerous issue is that if the highly rival state of Vaishali, Magadha's Emperor Bimbisara, knows about Ambapali, he won't hesitate to apply force and tricks against the state.
Member-I :	But Sir, Don't take seriously the messenger's news. We will wait and watch what they want.
Ganadhar :	Respected Members, we may be watchful and vigilant regarding the conditions of the external states, but what can be done about the internal situations?
Member-I :	Sir, I couldn't understand you.
Ganadhar :	You will be distressed and astonished to know that some of the aristocrats, Barons, of Vaishali and the esteemed members of the Council fight among themselves to marry Ambapali. If the internal conflicts of the state get heavier than the external invasion, the situation will be critical and challenging to manage.
Sheelabhadra :	It's understood from Ganadhar Sir's

	statements that Ambapali's beauty is the reason for both the external and internal conflicts outside and inside the state, respectively.
Member-I :	I also feel the same. Have you considered any remedy or solution for this, Ganadhar, Sir?

[Basumitra and Ambapali enter at that time.]

	Both of them paid respect to all the members present there.
Basumitra :	(Submissively) We have reached here immediately, as per the order of Hon'ble Chief Administrator Ganadhar Sir. What's the order for us?
Ganadhar :	Ambapali, some days earlier, we honoured you with the 'Best Dancer Award' of the State at this Conference Hall.
Ambapali :	I am grateful to you all!
Ganadhar :	But today, I am going to punish you.
Amba :	What's my crime?
Sheelabhadra :	Your celestial beauty is your crime. Sometimes, blessings to someone may be a curse to the public. That is what exactly happening today. To marry Ambapali, the entire state is clouded with the civil war.
Ambapali :	Respected Members of the Council! I should not be the cause of any controversy. I have been betrothed to someone.
Member-I :	Yes, you may be affianced, but you have yet to be married.

Ambapali	:	But why? Who are you to make this type of decision about me?
Ganadhar	:	I am the Head of the Autonomous State Council of Vaishali. The responsibility of State Governance is bestowed on me. I can take any decision, keeping in view the state's welfare for an individual or the community, as per the approval of the Council.
Basumitra	:	(Terrified) What kind of decision have you taken for my Amba?
Ganadhar	:	I have already decided that after the approval of the council members, it will be converted into law. Esteemed Members of the Council! Today, we have discussed the matter from different angles. Taking all this into account, I have decided that if Ambapali becomes the wife of an individual, the merchants and barons of the state will be unhappy, and their dissatisfaction will be a danger to the state of Vaishali.
Sheelabhadra	:	Well, you have publicly announced your decision regarding this matter.
Ganadhar	:	I want the public to have the right over Ambapali rather than an individual. She will be 'Vaishali's Courtesan'.
Ambapali	:	(Shouting) Courtesan!!!
Ganadhar	:	Yes, Courtesan. If anybody in the state wants, he can enjoy your company.
Ambapali	:	No, no; that can't be.

Member-I	:	(Happily) You have framed a new rule.
Ganadhar	:	No, Sir, this may be the first case for Vaishali state. Traditionally, this system has been practised and handed down from generation to generation in our adjoining states like Videha, Malla, and Kala. If the beauty of a woman becomes detrimental to the safety and security of the state, for the welfare of the state, she is declared as the 'Courtesan, a *Nagar Badhu* of the State'. Over her, the entire state will have the right. She can't be an individual's property. Thus, unnecessary fights among the wealthy and powerful people of the state can be avoided. Otherwise it may create chaotic situation in the state. I seek your views in this regard.
All members	:	(in Unison) We unanimously agree to your proposal.
Basumitra	:	A great injustice! Great injustice!! You can't make such a decision regarding my daughter.
Member-II	:	(Jokingly) Your daughter! (Laughter) You are not his father.
Basumitra	:	Sir! I am not her biological father, but she is more than my daughter.
Sheelabhadra	:	Alright. You will dedicate your daughter to the welfare of the state. As a good citizen of the state, you also have some responsibility.

Ambapali : (Angrily) It's only a farce and hypocrisy. As I am fatherless, the fostered daughter of an orchard's watchman, you teach us moral responsibilities. If a daughter or sister of any of you were in my place, would the Council take the same decision it declares today? (Seeing them silent) Please respond to my question. Why are you quiet?

Sheelabhadra : Ambapali! It's not of an individual's decision but of the Council.

Ambapali : I know, Sir. Some of you in the Council effortlessly fulfil your interest in the public's name.

Ganadhar : Be calm and quiet. We have already taken our decision. No changes can be made to that. But we are ready to accept your conditions if you lay before the council.

Ambapali : This is a meaningless statement to cover up the unjust decision you have already taken.

Member-I : You are going beyond your limits, Ambapali. If the Council wants, you can be given life-long imprisonment.

Ambapali : Imprisonment! (Laughter) If I am imprisoned, how will your carnal desires calm down? Please take it down, the esteemed members of the Council! The injustice you have made in the name of giving justice over a woman's birthright, for that, you have to pay a

	lot. This community will face the battle of bloodshed for the cruelty you have imposed in the name of democracy. It will be ruined one day.
Ganadhar :	No, no, Devi Ambapali! You should not curse like that. You are a member of the state. You should be thanked for the welfare of Vaishali State. We have to safeguard the state's democracy.
Sheelabhadra :	Ambapali, Why do you want to surrender your celestial beauty, gorgeous look, excellent lustre, and extraordinary personality before an ordinary person as his wife?
Member-II :	Yes, Devi Ambapali! As per the customary practices and traditional laws of the society, a woman surrenders her life to a man whom she gets married and becomes a maid until she breathes last. This is the life of an ordinary woman. But, you are an extra-ordinary woman jewel, a priceless jewel.
Ambapali :	(Sarcastically) According to you, this is the special status of life! I condemn this.
Ganadhar :	Devi Ambapali! We are donating the mango orchard where your father works as the watchman. You will be allotted the city's tallest apartment and hundreds of maidservants, elephants, horses, many chariots, etc., for your comfort. You will enjoy life and wealth like a king. To date,

	nobody else in Astakula of Bajisangh has availed this royal status. Neither the merchants nor the kings have ever wanted that.
Ambapali :	Do you think this is the price of my life?
Ganadhar :	No, Devi, you are a precious jewel. You are beyond the estimation of price. I, at this moment, also declare that nobody can force you for sensual gratification against your will. Even in any emergency throughout the state, no investigation can be made at your apartment for seven days if you don't want to.
Sheelabhadra :	What are you saying, Sir? You should not give her so much freedom. It may create problem for the state.
Ambapali :	You have never thought of what is right or wrong when you deprive someone of her freedom/ natural rights?
Member-I :	Yes, we have not discussed that, keeping in view the community's welfare.
Ambapali :	Is it for the welfare of the community or the greed and lustfulness of the affluent Merchants, Barons and esteemed Members of the Council?
Member-I :	Ganadhar, Sir, I strongly oppose this.
Ambapali :	If you condemn this with your highest energy level, the truth can be falsified. I have already understood your aims.
Ganadhar :	I can sense and feel your anguish, Devi,

	but following my requests, you think happily of the state's welfare. Vaishali is now plagued by danger from all directions. You will be the central point of this community. The sons of the Merchants and the Barons of this place will gratify their senses, earning pleasure and showing interest in you. You are the only one who can bind them in one thread. You are the excellent means to accomplish this work effortlessly…otherwise, being engrossed in the civil war will ruin the democracy of the Vaishali State.
Ambapali	: (Thoughtfully) All right. Then, Ganadhar Sir, please make aware the public of Vaishali that for the more significant interest and betterment of the state, from today onwards, Ambapali accepts the status and rights of the 'Courtesan', giving up her wifehood status of an individual.
Basumitra	: Amba, my daughter! Now all my hopes and dreams are shattered.
Ambapali	: Yes, Baba (Daddy)!

[She breaks down, and the members of the Council are speechless and looking downward.]

Scene-IV

[It's Ambapali's home. Soma enters from outside. He holds a basket of canes with a lid. He looks around. He gets surprised not to see anybody.]

Soma	:	Nobody is here. Where have they gone? Why the house seems to be dreary? (Looking inside) Uncle! Uncle!!

['Who?' is heard in the breaking voice from the house?]

Soma	:	I have come back, Uncle.
Basumitra	:	(He enters trembling.) O, Soma. Why did you return, my son?
Soma	:	(Being worried) What happened, Uncle? Why are you so weak now?
Basumitra	:	It's also a surprise how I do live. Why have I not died? God has allowed me to suffer.
Soma	:	Please, tell me everything frankly, Uncle. Where is Amba?
Basumitra	:	Amba is not with me; my daughter is not with me.
Soma	:	(Astonishingly) She is not here. What does this mean?
Basumitra	:	What can I do here, my son? She is sacrificed in the name of the state or country and the public.
Soma	:	Is Ambapali dead?
Basumitra	:	If she died, I would be happier than this state of life. Her death could have been better than her present state of life.
Soma	:	Please tell me where Amba is. What has happened to her?
Basumitra	:	It will be better if you don't listen to that.

Soma	:	No, no, you have to tell me. Ambapali is my fiancée and my would-be wife.
Basumitra	:	(Smiling) Wife! Daughter-in-law! She can't be anybody's wife. She can't be anybody's daughter-in-law too. Now she is the 'Bride of the City'. She is a Courtesan.
Soma	:	(With surprise) Courtesan!!
Basumitra	:	Yes, yes, Courtesan. Her beauty was the reason for her misfortune. It's a curse to her life. She has been victimized by the 'thirst of the public' in the name of democracy. Everybody desires her for sensual gratification.
Soma	:	But my marriage with Amba has been fixed.
Basumitra	:	You forget all that, my son; forget that. You forget that you ever met her. You see how I have forgotten…my daughter, my Amba…

[Trying to suppress his emotions, he enters the room.]

Soma	:	Will I forget? Will I forget Ambapali? She is my life; she is my dream. I promised her to return before the Full Moon Day, my darling…I have come back rightly. But where are you now? Please, come to see what I have brought for you at least once. (Opening the cane basket, he shows a necklace.) Amba, you see, this is my mother's necklace. Before she died, she stored it for her daughter-in-law.

Won't you wear this necklace once? ... Hey, you see the scarlet colour wrapper I have stitched for you carefully. It will look excellent on your curly black hair. I have imagined you as my new bride; it is heard that you can't be my wife at all... where are you now? I will try to bring you back. Yes, yes...I will...She is now the Courtesan!!! No, no, Amba is my fiancée. Who dared her to be the 'Courtesan of the State'? Is it the 'Board of Councillors' of Vaishali, the Group of Merchants, or the Class of Barons? No, no, all of them have conspired together for their self-interest against my would-be wife, who has been victimized now. I won't leave anyone. (Looking at his two hands helplessly) who will I take revenge upon? They are all the distinguished persons of the state; they have their wealth, power, force, and prestige...the rules of the state support them- what can I do alone? Or Can I forgive myself for this state of helplessness for my Amba? What shall I do now? (Lamenting)

ACT-III

Scene-I

[It is Ambapali's Luxury Hall of Entertainment. The maid Chapala supervises the decoration of the hall. Having heard the clamour outside, she goes out and comes in. Again, she goes out, keeping her eyes upon the hall. At this moment, well-clad and gorgeously decked Courtesan Ambapali enters the Hall of Entertainment. She unmindfully plays the lyre placed on the seat.]

Chapala	:	(Entering) Princess! The socially well-established people of Vaishali are waiting outside for your consent to enter. (Seeing Amba silent) What will I tell them?
Amba	:	Chapala, you deny them all. Today, I want to avoid meeting anybody.
Chapala	:	Among them are Ganadhar Sir, some Council members and the State General.
Amba	:	Whoever they may be, I won't meet anyone this day.
Chapala	:	As directed, I have denied them all saying your illness. Still, then, they are not listening to me. They are saying they don't have any objection if you don't perform

		any show; they have come to meet you only once.
Amba	:	Alright. Each one has to pay five hundred gold coins if they want to meet me. [Chapala leaves and again comes back.]
Chapala	:	They have all returned, keeping their faces downward, the supreme mistress.
Amba	:	(Smiling halfway) Chapala, have you visited the city today?
Chapala	:	Yes, my noble lady!
Amba	:	Is there any news?
Chapala	:	No, my noble lady. Your parents have yet to return from the pilgrimage.
Amba	:	Have you received any messages about them?
Chapala	:	No, I am still waiting for any information about them. I have repeated the same message before you.
Amba	:	Tell me once more…that story, their story.
Chapala	:	(Getting surprised) Her majesty! The day you entered the palace was spring's first full moon day. The entire Vaishali was active and vibrant in celebrating your arrival here. For your honour, the Merchants, the Barons, and the Councillors of the Royal Court got united here. When the palace was surcharged and reverberated with dancing, drinking and merry-making, your fiancé Soma returned to your home.

Amba	:	What happened then? (Shyly)
Chapala	:	When he heard everything about you at your home, he got depressed and distressed, too. He ran up to this palace. When the Aristocrats, Merchants, Barons, and Councillors were waiting eagerly outside for an appointment with you, why would the security personnel allow that poor guy to enter the palace? He returned.
Amba	:	Couldn't you pass the information to me?
Chapala	:	Observing his lunatic state, the security guard didn't feel good to inform you then.
Amba	:	What happened after that?
Chapala	:	For some days, people saw him playing the flute beneath a tree in the mango orchard. But one day, they marked the same flute lying on the ground of that tree. He is not there.
Amba	:	(Soliloquy) He is not there…
Chapala	:	Nobody knows where he has gone. But you have heard this story from me several times. Why do you want to listen to it again and again from me?
Amba	:	I want to fill the blank space of my heart hearing that tiny tale, Chapala.
Chapala	:	No, my noble lady! That blank space won't be in life forever. One day, someone will fill your heart's emptiness with the treasure of love. He will flood your lonely

		heart with love...all your anguish will get pacified and subsided, *Mahadei*.
Amba	:	Stop, Chapala...Don't say that story.
Chapala	:	One more information is about your friend Madhavi. I met her.
Amba	:	(Happily) Really? What did she tell?
Chapala	:	She has come to her father's house eight days earlier. Her husband and her son have accompanied her.
Amba	:	Husband! Son!! (Getting up overwhelmed)
Chapala	:	I told him about you! She knows everything. She is depressed for you. If we had not compelled her to participate in that 'Dance Programme', she would have stayed happily with her family members after marriage.
Amba	:	Could you not tell her to come here, Chapala?
Chapala	:	She said before I said to her, "I am interested in meeting Amba. But-"
Amba	:	But?
Chapala	:	Her husband stopped her from coming here.

[Without saying anything, Amba goes to stand near the window. A strange feeling is marked on her face. At a distance, the horse galloping with clops is heard.]

Amba	:	What's the time now at night?
Chapala	:	It's midnight now.

Amba	:	What's this? A horse galloping is heard. Who's coming this time?

[The Door Keeper enters to pass the message.]

Door Keeper	:	A foreigner has come. He wants to meet *Mahadei*.
Chapala	:	A foreigner! At mid-night!
Door Keeper	:	He says, "It has been late coming from a long distance."
Chapala	:	Does he know that he has to pay five hundred gold coins only to meet Devi Amba.
Door Keeper	:	He knows the conditions and is ready to pay one thousand gold coins. Again, he says he will return just after meeting the lady Amba.

[Chapala looks at Ambapali astonishingly.]

Amba	:	Invite him cordially with great honour. I am coming. (Exit)

[Chapala accompanies a tall man with a muscular physique.]

Foreigner	:	(Looking around) Only a few hours left for the night to end. I have to return after meeting lady Amba. Pass her the message to come fast.
Chapala	:	Please be seated.
Amba	:	(Entering) Why are you interested in returning so early?
Foreigner	:	(He stands up. In his look, there is a mixed feeling of happiness and wonder.) You are

what I imagined to be. O, celestial nymph! Your lotus-stalked hands, your red-petalled lotus-like lips, your incendiary golden waist, your pearl necklace shining on your milky neck, your curly black long chignon, your spotless moonlike face, etc, do always reflect and reverberate in my heart. By your bodily fragrance, all my senses are pleased and elevated today. A beautiful lamp of love gets kindled today in my sincere desire for lust.

Amba : (Facing downward with shyness) May I know you, please?

Foreigner : My introduction is unnecessary, O, my darling! I am your fan (Appreciator); I sincerely praise your talent in dancing, singing, and engagement in poetic discourse and beauty. I was determined to meet you at least once. I have got the chance today after a long time. You usually spend the first two quarters of the evening entertaining your guests at your Dancing Hall. Though I tried my best, I couldn't reach you. You pardon me, as I meet you at the midnight hour.

Amba : Have you come to this state for the first time?

Foreigner : I came here earlier once or twice. Then…

Amba : It seems to me that I have met you somewhere.

Foreigner : Have you seen me? How can it be?

Amba	:	(Try to recollect)…some years ago in the forest of Vaishali frontier, at the dusk when you had lost your path. You are, perhaps, that man, though I am not wrong.
Foreigner	:	(Looking at Amba's face) Yes, yes, I have remembered that incident. While Ambapali was tracing her memory before my eyes came naturally a nubile lady's indiscrete physique wandering in that forest. The heavenly beauty of that day is still stored intact in my heart. The black shade of disappointment lies only in her two blue-sea eyes. My dream girl, victimized by the royal conspiracy, has become the courtesan.
Amba	:	Please, stop talking any more. Tell me, "How can I help you?"
Foreigner	:	I want to see your feet vibrant dancing and hear your sweet, melodious voice while playing with the lyre. The heavenly nymph gorgeous beauty Ambapali of Vaishali is dancing before Magadha's… (He stops while saying.)
Amba	:	Are you from Magadha?
Foreigner	:	No, I have wrongly uttered the name of Magadha. Please start your dancing, Damsel, and calm down my thirst for many ages.
Amba	:	But, with one condition, I will start dancing.

Foreigner	:	I am ready to donate as many gold coins as you want.
Amba	:	I don't want to take a single coin of that.
Foreigner	:	Then…
Amba	:	I earnestly want to know your identity.
Foreigner	:	My identity! OK, alright. After I see your dance performance, I will disclose my identity. I accept your term.
Amba	:	Ok. I accept your request. [She starts performing dance with song and music.]

Love-sick I, the lotus bud, was in darkness; Secretly, someone came and whispered to my ears, "The sun has risen"; Like a river, I was meandering through the unknown desert; Someone brings to my front the address of the sea before I lose my direction; On my bluish water are blooming many lilies of different colours. Love-sick I…(She sang in her sweet melodious voice.)

Foreigner : (After the dance is over) Wonderful! Wonderful!! Marvellous is your art of dancing all over the world. O, Damsel! You seemed to me a celestial nymph while you danced. Like magnolia is your soft white body…like the morning star is your lustrous face along with your every expression, hand postures, the wavy movement of your waist and the divinely gracious feel is perceived in your artistic

	performance. I felt as if I were dancing on sea waves, on the ripples of the breeze; on the infinite blue sky, I was floating away to the unfathomed horizon, far away… where there is no sorrow, no unhappiness, no attachments of the earth…in a heavenly bliss I have been wholly engrossed.
Amba	: Sir, you are not an ordinary person who gets engrossed in artistic performances; you are but indeed an artist of a higher order.
Foreigner	: I? I am not an artist? No, no.
Amba	: Then, who are you?
Foreigner	: I will tell, Amba. But, you will drive me away from this place after you know my identity. So, before that, let me spend some time more with you.
Amba	: No, Sir. Amba will never humiliate her guest. Be sure, your identity will not be disclosed.
Foreigner	: I am Emperor Bimbisara.
Amba	: (Astonishingly) Emperor Bimbisara! Emperor of Magadha!!
Bimbisara	: Yes, Ambapali, I am the Emperor of Magadha, and your lover. I started to love you secretly after I heard about you. But, when I was out of control, I disguised myself to meet you, inviting all the dangers and complications in my life.
Amba	: You are Vaishali's adversary, my state's enemy.

Bimbisara	:	Yes, I am the enemy of Vaishali, but not yours.
Amba	:	Maharaj! How can it be, Maharaj? You are the enemy of my state.
Bimbisara	:	There's no distinction between friend and enemy before Amba's love. I want you… If anybody knows about my stay here, Do you know what my consequence will be, Amba?
Amba	:	Emperor!
Bimbisara	:	If you want, you can help the enemy of the country be caught hold of.

[Repeated knocks on the door].

Amba	:	Chapala! See who is knocking. (Chapala goes out, and Amba looks through the window and gets shocked.) Emperor! Please, come quickly, and hide yourself inside my bedroom.

[Ambapali and the Emperor move inside, and the General of Vaishali and Chapala enter.]

General	:	(Looking around) Where is Devi, Ambapali?
Chapala	:	She is sleeping in the bedroom. At this unusual time, …
General	:	Yes, I have an emergency talk with her now. Inform her quickly.
Amba	:	(Entering) Who's there, Chapala?
General	:	I say 'Pranam' to Devi Ambapali.
Amba	:	Who? O, the Reverend General.

General	:	Devi, I had to come on a special duty.
Amba	:	What's that special work? Couldn't you wait for the next day?
General	:	Devi, I heard from the messenger that a foreigner was a guest for you at midnight. Is it true?
Amba	:	You don't have the right to ask any question about that to me.
General	:	I know that. But, the news is that the Emperor of Magadha has secretly entered Vaishali. This kind of alertness and vigilance is administered.
Amba	:	He is not from Magadha.
General	:	You don't know that he is cruel, insolent and the most dangerous enemy of Vaishali, the Emperor Bimbisara. He had frequently entered this city disguised earlier. Let me see him at least once.
Amba	:	No.
General	:	Then, I have to disobey your order forcefully.
Amba	:	You need to remember, the General; if you don't get the permission of Ambapali, you have to wait outside for seven days to make any investigation of her residence.
General	:	(Being agitated) It's all right. But, you don't forget that you are being a traitor to allow an enemy of the state to shelter at your residence.

Amba	:	I need more time to listen to your alert message. You may go now. Yes, you can inform your Councillors, Merchants, and Barons not to meet me for seven days from this day.

[The General leaves.]

Scene-II

[This is Ambapali's Hall of Residence. Ambapali plays with the strings of the lyre, and Bimbisara sits.]

Bimbisara	:	Ambapali! It has already been seven days since I stayed at your residence. One more night is left for me to go. After that, the Emperor of Magadha will be imprisoned, and capital punishment will result from entering the enemy state without permission.
Amba	:	(Closing the Emperor's face with her hands) No, Maharaj, I won't allow you to die.
Bimbisara	:	(Laughing) Are you afraid of, darling? You see, I don't have fear at all. I have received your love; I don't desire any more. Had it not happened like this, how would I get the time to spend for seven more days at a stretch? I don't have any obsession right now, my darling.
Amba	:	Emperor! But I can't live with the obsession of losing you. You have brought happiness to my empty life. I knew well, "One can

		love young virgin Amba, but nobody to the Courtesan." Here, everybody wants my beautiful body at the cost of money. Today, you have won me by your love. I am not mine. I am yours only; yours only.
Bimbisara	:	Amba, my Darling! The tiny space I have occupied at your heart is more valuable than King's throne of Magadha. Come, my love! Let the rest part of this last night be spent with your intimacy.
Amba	:	Emperor! You won't be more emotional right now. Think of the strategy with which you can escape secretly from this spot…If you are alive, this unfortunate woman can get an opportunity to meet you one day…If we don't meet again in future, I will spend the rest of my life with the memory of these last days.
Bimbisara	:	Amba! (Getting Overwhelmed)
Amba	:	(Being cautious) Chapala! (Chapala enters) Is there no other way to get out of the palace, Chapala?
Chapala	:	My noble lady! The soldiers are deployed around the palace. The General and other Councillors are vigilant to control and direct the situation. All the paths to enter and exit the palace are blocked.
Amba	:	No, all the paths can't be blocked. Any one of the paths must be open. There is a need for tricks and intelligence to search for that.

Chapala	:	Yes Madam! The councillors are especially aggrieved. Barring them, you were entertaining the King of the enemy state. They are waiting for the night to end.
Amba	:	Chapala, you listen to me! (Chapala shows a different reaction while Amba whispers to her.)
Chapala	:	I move now. I will execute your plan.
Bimbisara	:	Amba! As I have received your hospitality here, the councillors, the Merchants, the Barons, and the public have been highly outraged. It's also natural. If I escape anyhow from this place, I can live. If they don't find me, they will punish you cruelly. I can't leave the place putting you in trouble. Instead, let them come; if they kill the Emperor of Magadha, history will speak that the most potent tyrannical ruler of Magadha, Bimbisara, lost his life for love.
Amba	:	You want to be immortal like this, Emperor! (Laughing) No, no, please, you return to your state. The army of Vaishali is strong. If any battle is to be fought in future, you may breathe your last bravely. I can't allow the General to capture you from my chamber without fight. This will be an insult to Vaishali's bravery.
Bimbisara	:	(Smiling) You are so confident in your army.
Amba	:	Certainly.

Chapala	:	(Entering) Everything is ready, *Mahadei*.
Amba	:	Emperor! Please, you come. It won't be right to stay here for a while.
Bimbisara	:	But, My Love...if anything happens to you...
Amba	:	You don't worry about me at all. If they don't find the Emperor of Magadha in my chamber, on what ground will they punish me? Without any proof, no one can be punished in the *sangha*-governed states. Please move with Chapala without wasting time; she will help you understand everything.
Bimbisara	:	It's OK. I am leaving, my darling. Though I leave you physically, my heart, mind, and soul are with you. You can do what you want with that.

[Chapala and Bimbisara leave.]

Amba	:	(She glances over the path the Emperor treads. She talks to herself.) What a strange state I have plunged into! My hope to marry Soma was shattered when I had been publicly declared 'the Courtesan of the State' for the state's welfare. Since that day, I have disliked the males. Humiliating them, I was enjoying. But what has happened to me this day? How come from the clay-bed of hate stored in my heart blossoms a hundred petalled lotus of love...how irresistible zeal for love arises in me...but, he is the enemy

of my state...Can the ordinary people of Vaishali forgive me for this? No, but what can I do? Can anyone love taking into account the enmity, friendship, casteism, class, creed and complexion? Love, like the melodious voice of the cuckoo, *phalguna*'s colour, the breeze of the spring season, the loosely slackened black clouds of the Rainy season, and the white lilies of autumn sprouts naturally in the human heart. It gets dyed in a hundred colours and a hundred musical rhythms play in the heart. It does not wait for anybody's decision or the social rules and restrictions.

[Ganadhar, the General and the Watchman enter.]

Amba : (Her unmindfulness gets disrupted.) Is the seven-day restriction over, General Sir?

General : Watchman! Pass my order to the soldiers. Without wasting a moment, investigate each nook and corner of the palace to find out and imprison the wicked Emperor.

Amba : (Calmly) Ganadhar, Sir, please be seated; why you are standing? They need time to investigate. You can sit, please, General Sir. Isn't the seven-day wait excruciating?

General : Are you joking?

Amba : No, not at all. How can I crack jokes on you? Instead, I feel humiliated because of the accusation of hiding any Emperor at my palace.

General	:	Do you know who he is? But, you are entertaining him for seven days.
Amba	:	The State Council Board has instructed me only for entertainment. Can I disobey that order?
General	:	Does it mean to be with the state's enemy?
Amba	:	(in commanding voice) I don't know who is an enemy or a friend to whom. Anybody can be intimate with me if he pays me a wholesome amount. I do not usually decide whether he is a friend or a foe.
Ganadhar	:	Is it your responsibility to intentionally hide Magadha's Emperor in your palace?
Amba	:	Ganadhar Sir! Magadha's Emperor is not the pearl necklace for my neck or the small bracelet for my hands that can be concealed in the cane basket.
Watchman	:	(Entering) Sir! We carefully investigated every nook and corner of the palace, the garden, the cowshed, and the horse stable, but we couldn't find anybody.
Amba	:	Ganadhar Sir! Will you go to verify?
Ganadhar	:	Are you joking? Do you know what will be the consequence?
Amba	:	Punishment? Of what crime will I be punished?
General	:	Why didn't you allow anybody to investigate your palace before seven days?

Amba	:	That's not my crime, but my right. Is not that the Council of Vaishali granted me this right? Have I committed any crime?
General	:	But for the state's safety and security, I also have some right to ask you questions.
Amba	:	Have I ever told you that you don't have the right? You can ask.
General	:	For whom were you dancing and singing for the last seven days in your Hall of Entertainment without allowing anybody of our state to enter the palace? Who was that midnight guest?
Amba	:	General Sir! Firstly, I have a personal reason for not allowing anybody from the state to enter my palace. That can't be revealed. Secondly, I earn my livelihood through dancing and singing. Every day, I rehearse in the presence or absence of the public, only to entertain my clients later. There is a last question. But you can't force me to disclose the identity of that mid-night guest. Earlier, with the requests of many guests, I did not disclose their identities. (Looking at Ganadhar Sir meaningfully) Sir, I can reveal the name or identity if you direct me.
Ganadhar	:	No, no, these are your personal matters. Nobody can compel you. Let's move, General.
General	:	OK, all right. That shrewd Bimbisara has escaped today; one day, he will be caught.

Amba	:	Anyway, you have got an easy way to get hold of the Emperor of Magadha. Thank you for your bravery.
General	:	Ambapali!
Amba	:	General! I will complain about you to the Council for breaking my peaceful night and accusing me without proof.
Ganadhar	:	Please come, General. [Ganadhar and General leave the place while Amba laughs sarcastically.]

Scene-III

[It's the Councillor's Room of Magadha. The Emperor Bimbisara strolls agitatedly, and his chief minister looks at him silently.]

Chief Minister	:	Oh King! I want to tell you something if you permit me to do so.
Bimbisara	:	There is no need for permission. You can say, my minister. You have complete freedom to advise the King at any time.
Chief Minister	:	Oh King! You can pardon me for my boldness. You should not have entered the enemy state without protection. It's unsuitable for a dutiful king to be dwindled with any youthful imprudence. Had anything happened to you,…
Bimbisara	:	The Emperor of Magadha knows very well how to defend himself.
Chief Minister	:	But…Ambapali's intelligence has saved

	you. It is my request to our king that the same sort of incident may not be repeated.
Bimbisara :	But...
Chief Minister:	But why, My Lord? Can't you restrain yourself to a Courtesan's attraction? There is a reasonable number of beautiful dancers at your Royal Court. The empress also gets very worried waiting for you days and nights at the inner apartment.
Bimbisara :	Who said this to you?
Chief Minister:	The queen Kshema herself has expressed her anxiety before me.
Bimbisara :	How did she know?
Chief Minister:	Oh King! The queen Kshema is Vaishali's daughter. She is concerned about the hostility between these two states. You should pay attention to her mental state,...
Bimbisara :	There won't be any reason for her to express her anxiety. Vaishali will never be our enemy state but a small part of our vast Empire of Magadha.
Chief Minister :	Then, you...

(The General enters.)

General :	I congratulate you, My Lord!
Bimbisara :	General, please come. Can you guess for which reason have I called you here?
General :	Whatever the reason may be, I am prepared to shed every drop of my blood to execute the King's order.

Bimbisara	:	But, if the Kingship of the *Shishunaga* Dynasty is not achieved, then Bimbisara's birth in this dynasty will be useless, and your commandership of the army of Magadha will also be meaningless.
General	:	Your wishes will be fulfilled, Oh King! If the Magadha empire expands to the south sea, we must defeat the King of Avanti and Mathura, Anantabarmana. But I know that our King's interest is to invade Vaishali. So, let Vaishali be invaded first. I request Maharaj; if Vaishali's democracy is to be shattered, we have to invade the states like Malla, Shakya, and Kashikoliya simultaneously. The Administrative Office of Magadha's Capital is to be transferred to Vaishali. Then, Vaishali will be the central point of our administration.
Bimbisara	:	(Happily) General, I knew you would understand my clear-cut visions well. Please start the preparations to execute our plans.
General	:	As you wish, My Lord! (Exit)
Bimbisara	:	Mahamantri! I have called you to the Council Hall to inform you of our plans. Do you have any say in it?
Chief Minister	:	I welcome your steps from the political point of view, Maharaj. But, for a Courtesan, if the King takes this decision, then my plea will be to you to reconsider the matter once more. I leave now. (He leaves after greeting.)

Bimbisara	:	(Soliloquy) How can I help you understand that Ambapali is not a dancer only; she is the tutelary deity residing in Bimbisara's heart and the soul of his being? I will grant the Courtesam Amba the status of my wife...but I know that Vaishali State will never approve my proposal. Vaishali consistently disregards the vastness and power of Magadha and criticizes Magadha's kingship in the name of the *Sangha*-based administration. My indifference towards them is termed as my weakness. Today, the Magadha emperor Bimbisara won't be indifferent to Vaishali. He won't hesitate to ruin it to fulfill his hopes and dreams.

[Bimbisara's sword gets unsheathed along with the musical concert of war.]

Scene-IV

[Ambapali is sitting in depression in her Hall.]

Chapala	:	(Entering hurriedly) Mahadei! Have you heard the news of today's battle?
Amba	:	Is there any new incident in the battle?
Chapala	:	Today, the 'Day of Rest' is declared for the battle.
Amba	:	Truly, Chapala?
Chapala	:	Yes, *Mahadei*; The Emperor has accepted Vaishali's 'Treaty Proposal'.

Amba	:	But, the loss of lives, bloodshed, the distressed cry of the wounded soldiers, destruction of wealth and properties, etc., happened only for me; only for me, Chapala.
Chapala	:	No, Mahadei, you are not responsible for all this. You have not persuaded the Magadha's Emperor to raise a battle.
Amba	:	Still, everybody knows the reason for this battle. Will they not accuse me and hold responsible for the loss of public property?
Chapala	:	Don't think you are responsible for this. It's not your fault. The first blunder of the Council is that they declared you as the 'Courtesan' for the welfare of the state upon whom the public has the right. If they had apprehended you as the cause of conflicts inside and outside the state for your celestial beauty, their first responsibility was to conduct your marriage ceremony immediately. Then, anybody would have hesitated to use force against a married woman. But, for their self-gratification, the administrators of Vaishali had to atone for the crime they committed against you. You did no wrong. You are not responsible for this war and bloodshed.
Amba	:	Yes, Chapala! You are right. Why will I be responsible for this battle? It has been a common tradition that male-dominated society always blames women as the root

of all evil. But they have forgotten that their lust invites all kinds of complications to our social life. Beauty is God's grace. Man's greed for that blessing gets transformed into a curse. They are responsible for all kinds of social degradation. Still, had I been able to resist emperor's love for me. Had I not loved Emperor Bimbisara, I would have rejected his love.

Chapala : Could you have done that?

Amba : Why couldn't I? I am the Courtesan of Vaishali. Who had authorized me the right to love the Magadha's Emperor?

Chapala : The Almighty has granted you that right. Human being's hearts are far above geographical boundaries, political conspiracies, caste disparities, and social barriers. It's very natural for the heart to love.

Amba : Chapala! Have you ever loved anyone? If I can do something for you, I will feel that my life is meaningful to reduce your plights to some extent.

Chapala : Her majesty! What can be more painful than not to get the most loved person?

Bimbisara : (Entering) If the beloved person requests the celestial nymph to stay with her, will she allow?

Amba : (Surprisingly) Emperor, you are here!! [Chapala goes inside.]

Bimbisara	:	Yes, my darling, Amba! There is no need to visit you secretly. The Magadha's King won't wait for the night's darkness to meet his beloved. No power of Vaishali can forbid me.
Amba	:	O' King, you have created such a vast uproarious battle for this. You have ruined the amassed wealth of this land. You have not done anything right for an ordinary woman like me.
Bimbisara	:	'What's right or wrong?' is decided by the sages, saints, and the learned men. What the King desires is right. There is nothing wrong in it. I know that you have been distressed by the destruction of Vaishali. What could I have done? There was no other way for me. I didn't think of any other plan when the State Council of Vaishali rejected my proposal to get 'my love'.
Amba	:	You are the King. You couldn't control your desire like an ordinary man.
Bimbisara	:	The King is also an ordinary man, my beloved. But the difference is that the King doesn't accept defeat so easily, whereas the ordinary man submissively embraces his defeat against fate. Amba! I thought you would be happy. Having seen the reaction to the injustice raised against you, you will be satisfied…But…
Amba	:	(Half-smiling) Anyway, leave it, Sir! You

		are tired; you need rest. Please come; Chapala must have arranged everything for you.
Bimbisara	:	No, Amba; I am not tired. In my blood lies the thirst for battle.
Amba	:	But in your heart?
Bimbisara	:	In the heart? You are only in my heart. Devi Ambapali is the tutelary deity of my heart.
Amba	:	Only in your heart empire? Not at any other place?
Bimbisara	:	(Understanding hints) My beloved! Until now, you were only the Goddess of love for me. Today, King Bimbisara will make you sit with him as the Empress of the vast kingdom.
Amba	:	(Overwhelming) Oh King!
Bimbisara	:	Yes, My love, you will be my queen who can sit with me on the throne of Magadha's Kingdom.
Amba	:	Queen of Magadha, the great empire! The *Patarani* of the Empress! …no…no…
Bimbisara	:	What happened, Amba? Why are you so much disturbed?
Amba	:	No, no, you should not make a blunder considering the courtesan as your wife.
Bimbisara	:	I have told you once that the King doesn't care right or wrong. What he desires will be done.

Amba	:	But you can't force me.
Bimbisara	:	Amba!
Amba	:	Yes, Emperor, you can't compel me to be your wife.
Bimbisara	:	But why do you have an objection to the proposal?
Amba	:	Objection, yes…Since I love you, I can't make a significant loss to you. Oh King, nobody will accept a Courtesan as the Queen of Magadha.
Bimbisara	:	They will be forced to accept.
Amba	:	Because of the fear for the King, perhaps they will accept it, but none of them will heartily approve of the relationship that I know. I don't want to create a black chapter in the historical chronicles of the Royal Dynasty of Magadha.
Bimbisara	:	OK, all right. If you wish this, giving up Magadha's throne, I am ready to live with you like an ordinary man.
Amba	:	*Oh King!* How are you saying this? Will you give up the throne for me?
Bimbisara	:	If the King declares something, he never withdraws from it.
Amba	:	But why?
Bimbisara	:	Why 'but' again? I agree with all your proposals.
Amba	:	O' King! When I decided to be the courtesan, I had accepted the public's

		right upon me since that day. The 'public' is not only of the State Council but of the entire state. How can I be an individual? The public of Vaishali may oppose to this. It's against the rule.
Bimbisara	:	(Angrily) Rule, rule, rule. Why do you put strange arguments before me? Where were those rules when one's fiancée gets converted to a Courtesan? Why did the people of your country not oppose this decision? I am not ready to accept any rule. I can take you forcefully with me.
Amba	:	Will you exercise power upon me?
Bimbisara	:	(Shockingly) No, Amba, no. I can't do anything against your will. I love you. While the most influential people of the state and outside eagerly wait for shelter at the insolent Ruler of Magadha, the Emperor himself takes shelters with you.
Amba	:	I am happy and think myself a fortunate one.
Bimbisara	:	No, you have made me happy. I am glad that Devi Ambapali, who is mainly desired by all, has loved me. Amba, please accept one more request of mine. Give me a chance to marry you and make you my Principal Queen.
Amba	:	No, Emperor, that can't be.
Bimbisara	:	Don't you love me?
Amba	:	I am ready to face the test you want to take

		to prove my love for you. But, to marry you,…
Bimbisara	:	Don't worry, my darling; I am not forcing you to decide now. You can take as much time as you want. The Magadha's Emperor will never lose his patience in this regard. He can wait for you until he breathed last. I leave now.
Amba	:	Will you return so early without taking some rest?
Bimbisara	:	Yes, darling, I must arrange for the wounded people in the battle. I have been away from the capital for many a day, so I must inspect the situation. I will return soon… That visit will be my last visit to this place.
Amba	:	(Getting shocked) Why my lord?
Bimbisara	:	(Smiling) After that, you will spend every moment with me as my wife in Magadha. I won't come here again. Yes, please be prepared to leave the place early. I am going now, my darling.
Amba	:	I say *pranam* to you, My Lord. (Bimbisara straightens Amba while she bends downward to touch his feet out of respect. He looks at her calmly and closely. He cajoles her head for a while and leaves. Ambapali looks at his departure.)
Chapala	:	(Entering) O' my mistress! Why the King returned so early? When will he come again?

Amba	:	Yes, he will come to take me as his Principal Queen after marrying me.
Chapala	:	Truly? What can be happier than this? God is so compassionate.
Amba	:	No, Chapala, God is very cruel. He gets amused in colouring one's heart with hopes and shattering those hopes. In my early youth, I dreamt of becoming the wife of someone… suddenly that dream was shattered…then I became a courtesan of the state'…Suppressing a woman's desire inside, when I am trying to accept my futile and purposeless life, my beloved person came to my life. Now he wants to marry me and give the status of the first queen…But, how can I accept his proposal, Chapala?
Chapala	:	Why can't you?
Amba	:	No, Chapala…I can't; who can be more unfortunate than me? (Crying)
Chapala	:	When the King is ready to marry you, why can't you do so? Nobody can obstruct you in this Vaishali city.
Amba	:	I know, Chapala…but conflict doesn't lie outside…it is within me. Being the Principal Queen of Magadha, I can't make the King's throne dirty and sinful. I can't ruin the Royal Dynasty of Magadha for my self-interest. *Maharaj* can't understand this. He is mad in my love. He can suppress others' voices and force them to be silent,

	but for how many days? Apart from that, I can't betray my state, Vaishali. I can't be disloyal to my mother land.
Chapala	: O' my mistress! Vaishali has betrayed you, insulted you and shattered your dreams. She has taken away your right to live like a respectable woman like others.
Amba	: But Vaishali is my mother. I am still determining who my mother is. This land has nourished and nurtured me. Her air and water helped me grow up here. Today, it will be a great insult to the land of Vaishali if I get married to the person who was involved in bloodshed here. To leave this land after marriage is an insult to it.
Chapala	: You are getting unnecessarily emotional. No one thinks of others so profoundly. Your story will be a matter of discussion for some days. All the people will forget after that.
Amba	: But I can't forget, Chapala…I can't. I can never forgive myself for this work.
Chapala	: But the King!
Amba	: (Getting Overwhelmed) Yes, Emperor Bimbisara, the greatest enemy of Vaishali, but he is the ruler of my heart…in my every particle of my blood, Bimbisara is inscribed…Bimbisara. (Like a lunatic, she laughs and subsequently gets broken by heart heavily. Chapala gets worried.)

Scene-V

[On the road of Vaishali, a *Bauddha Bhikshu* (Buddhist monk) walks, holding a begging bowl and saying, 'Give me alms'. The people walking on the road stay a while and pay respect to him'. The mendicant blesses them all. From the opposite side, Ambapali comes.]

Amba : I bow down to you.

Monk : Bless you.

[Ambapali puts her pearl necklace on the *bhikshu's* begging bowl after removing it from her neck.]

What do you do, *Maa* (out of respect)? I can't receive this gift.

Amba : Why monk?

Monk : There is restriction in our *Sangha* to receive any precious gift.

Amba : But you have not asked for it. Why there is an objection for receiving what is gifted spontaneously?

Monk : No, my noble lady, please remove your gift from my bowl. When one is satisfied with some food, what will he do with this precious gift?

Amba : O' holy monk! You can throw the gift somewhere you like. Because, Ambapali never takes back the alms which she gives.

Monk : (Getting surprised) Ambapali!

Ambapali : Do you know me, O' monk!

Monk : No, no…

Amba	:	A monk can't tell a lie.
Monk	:	No, it's not a lie. Perhaps I knew the young girl Amba some years back, but not the courtesan Ambapali.
Amba	:	Who are you? What's your name?
Monk	:	What's the need of knowing the name of a monk? I am only a monk, nothing else.
Amba	:	But you can't hide your identity, Soma. I have recognized you rightly from your 'shaven head' and orange-coloured dress.
Amba	:	Yes, you have correctly identified me. But now I don't take any identity. I am a monk only.
Amba	:	Soma, where have you been for so long? Don't you think of me at all? Haven't you ever desired to come and see me how I am?
Monk	:	(Angrily) What could I see? How is my fiancée engrossed in entertainment with other males? What to see? To see my fiancée entertaining the different males being a courtesan?
Amba	:	Soma!
Monk	:	(Getting composed) No, honourable lady (out of respect to a lady)! Please forgive me. A monk should not utter these words. I have gone against the rules. O *Tathagata* (Lord Buddha)! Please forgive me.
Amba	:	You would rather condemn me, Soma, but

		don't show your cruelty towards me. You know well how I have been victimized in the name of 'Democracy'. I had no other way.
Monk	:	It will be a sin for a monk if he is engaged in any discourse other than *Dharma*. Please take your gift back from me. O blessed one, take back your gift. I can't take this.
Amba	:	Listen to me, I have told you I never take back my gift. Take it; it can be helpful to your association.
Monk	:	O, lady! You hear me; having received the gift from a prostitute like you is unholy and sinful.
Amba	:	But, to receive compassion from this courtesan, the Kings, Merchants, and Barons in this country and abroad wait anxiously like the pied cuckoo in the rainy season. The jingling sound of my anklets once started, and many pearls get stored at my feet; with a slight coaxing, many crowns touch my feet…but you are a poor monk.
Monk	:	Stupid woman! The pride of wealth and youth has made you dull and ignorant. How many days will you be with your celestial beauty?
Amba	:	Stop delivering this moral lesson. You are forgetting, "Standing on the soil of Vaishali, you are talking to the Courtesan, Ambapali."

Monk	:	No, I have remembered that I am talking to an idol made up of bone, blood, and flesh that will one day be inflicted with old age, diseased and leave the world permanently.

[Amba gets shocked. While she becomes conscious of herself, Monk leaves the place. She picks up the pearl necklace from the ground and looks at the vast sky. The stage light is off.]

Scene-VI

[Lord Buddha sits on a raised platform in Vaishali's mango orchard. The *Bhikshus* (mendicants) are standing in his front.]

Monk	:	O' lightened one! Please tell us something about the nature of sorrow.
Buddha	:	O, monks! sorrow is the real truth. Birth is sorrow; old age is sorrow; disease is sorrow; death is sorrow; friendship is sorrow; separation is also sorrow. The preventive path to all these sorrows is the noble truth. It is eight in number.

[Another Buddhist monk enters.]

Monk	:	My Lord! The Courtesan of Vaishali, Ambapali, awaits you outside in the orchard. She tells us, "She won't leave the place unless you allow her to meet you."
Others	:	A courtesan will meet Lord Buddha! Let her return.

Buddha	:	O, monk! Let her come in.
Monk	:	Tathagataa! How are you doing this? Her presence will make the place unholy. She is a fallen woman, a harlot, and a prostitute.
Buddha	:	O' monk, there is a need for solid meditation for you. Refrain from earning knowledge only through doubts. Try to identify the 'true nature' of human beings.

[Ambapali enters and bows down to Lord Buddha.]

Amba	:	O, the most compassionate Lord, Tathagata Buddha! The most fallible woman, the prostitute is before you.
Buddha	:	Get up, Ambapali; nobody is fallen in the world. If one wears a red-coloured gown with a shaven head, he can't be a real monk, or the one who wears costly garments and leads a wealthy and aristocratic life can be mean. Everything depends on their holiness. Your mind is sanctified, so you are with a pure, sacred soul.
Amba	:	(Being overwhelmed) Lord! Please help me remove my sorrows, plights, miseries and sins. (Buddha assured her and blessed her.) Please listen to my prayer if you allow me to shelter at your feet.
Buddha	:	What's your prayer?
Amba	:	Lord! Please accept the mango orchard I have on the outskirts of this city

	compassionately. The sacred speeches of Lord Buddha may reverberate in the atmosphere of that orchard.
Buddha	: Let your wishes be fulfilled, O' noble lady.
Amba	: Lord! One more request I have. Because of your grace, my life has become. Tomorrow, please have your lunch with all other monks at my palace.
Buddha	: I accept your invitation, O' noble lady.
Amba	: Lord! You have unending compassion for me.
	[She leaves. Looking at her path, the Aristocrats enter. They pay respect to Lord Buddha.]
Buddha	: (He blesses.) Can I know your names, please?
Sheelabhadra	: Lord! I am Sheelabhadra, one member of Vaishali's Council Board; next to me is Ganadhar, Chief Administrator of the city; they are all the Merchants and Barons of Vaishali. All of us have come to you with a special request.
Buddha	: May I know your plea, please?
Sheelabhdra	: Tomorrow, for your honour at the Reception Hall of the State Council, there is an arrangement of a feast for you. Our request to you is that you all can have your lunch with us and make our lives blessed.
Buddha	: I am glad to hear from you, but...

All	:	What is the reason for your hesitation, O' Lord! We have arranged everything.
Buddha	:	I have already accepted an invitation for tomorrow's lunch before you reach out.
Ganadhar	:	Who's that lucky person? Whose invitation has Tathagata already accepted? For that he rejects our request.
Buddha	:	Before you come here, Ambapali has already invited me.
All	:	(Getting shocked) Ambapali! Have you accepted her invitation?
Buddha	:	Yes, I have accepted her plea.
Sheelabhadra	:	Lord, you don't know that she is an illegitimate child without any identity and the courtesan of the city.
Buddha	:	I don't need anybody's parental identity and social establishment. Before me, all are equal.
Ganadhar	:	Your presence at Ambapali's palace will be criticized by the people of Vaishali.
Monk	:	How do you dare to teach Tathagata what is right or wrong?
Ganadhar	:	It's my mistake, Lord. Still, give this matter a second thought. When all the Merchants, Barons, and councillors of the Royal Court of Vaishali hope for your kind presence to feast at the Conference Hall tomorrow, you will have lunch at an ordinary Courtesan's palace.

Buddha	:	Who is mean or great is beyond the comprehension of an ordinary man. I have accepted Ambapali's invitation. I can't withdraw my word. You all can return now.

[Buddha meditates- all look at each other in astonishment. The stage lights are off.]

Scene-VII

[Now, Ambapali is in her Hall of Residence. Absorbed in thoughts, she holds a stylus in her hand...she writes with an interval. Chapala comes in.]

Chapala	:	My noble lady! Some hours are left for the night to end...you are yet to sleep. You have not had your dinner tonight. If you neglect your body, the lovely lotus-like face will wither. In one night, your eyes get blackened. What are you writing sitting there? You can sleep for a while for the rest of the night.
Amba	:	How can I sleep, Chapala? Until now, there was a never ending night for me, a deep dark night. After a long time, the divine moment of a new sunrise has reached me. I can't miss that moment for sleep. Now can I deny the sunrise in the morning, closing my eyes? Can I reject light?
Chapala	:	What are you saying, my lady? I can't understand.

Amba	:	I couldn't understand all this earlier. Love, desire, greed, sexual gratification, marriage, separation, and motherhood seemed to me as mainly the objectives of life…there was nothing more than this beyond one's reach…there was nothing more to receive. All these desires are shot in my heart like arrows. Today, my heart gets released naturally from its pains and plights. My heart overflows with celestial bliss. Chapala, you go to sleep. I have to prepare myself for the sunrise in the darkness of my life.
Chapala	:	Don't worry. I have arranged everything for the following day. For Lord Buddha and his five hundred disciples, the best arrangement of food and rest is at the largest hall of the palace. In the morning, food items will be prepared.
Amba	:	(Smiling) I know, Chapala. Because of you, this vast palace, immense wealth, hundreds of male and maidservants, and stable for horses, elephants, etc, are all well-taken care of. I know that you must have finished all kinds of arrangements. But I have to do something. I have to arrange some costly gifts for Lord Buddha.
Chapala	:	What will you prepare, my lady? You will find many precious wealthy gifts in your storehouse, such as gemstones, pearls, gold, and diamond pieces. Extraordinary objects from this land and foreign land

		are stored. What you are lacking…the wealth of the sea will also dim here. What you want can be poured at Lord Buddha's feet.
Amba	:	The person whom you want me to gift is the Lord of all these wealth and properties of the world. What wealth can I gift him? I will gift Him a small gift of the feelings of my heart.
Chapala	:	What's that?
Amba	:	(Showing the birch leaves) You see what I have prepared in my sleepless night… hey, what has happened…Will you listen to what I have written down?
Amba	:	(Reading the birch leave)

Curly black hair, plugged with flowers, is surrounded by bees;

An unsteady deer's restless look, full of intoxicating love, has dimmed.

New leaves' colour, sweet, brings thrills to the lips,

The skilled artist has made in their hands the beautiful white body;

With the cold touch of death

It will untimely leave the world.

| Chapala | : | You have expressed some inauspicious signs in your writing. Why are you thinking of death from now on? That is far away from you. It's the time for you |

	to enjoy. You are getting overwhelmed unnecessarily. Instead, you rest as only a few hours are left until the night ends.
Amba :	(As if being hypnotized) No, Chapala, is there any end to sensual gratification? Is there any end to happiness? The desire for sex frequently adds ghee to the fire burning ever within the body. How do you know that death is at a long distance from you? Who can say when it will come to us? You go now, Chapala;...Let me stay alone for a while.

[Ambapali sits absorbed. The shade of internal conflicts is marked on her face. The stage light gets dimmed. It is seen that, from one side of the stage, Bimbisara enters.]

Bimbisara :	(In overwhelming voice) Amba, my darling! You come to my breast, and I have extended it here for you. I will deeply embrace you forever.

[Ambapali, being hypnotized, moves towards Bimbisara. From the other side of the stage enters Lord Buddha.]

Buddha :	This relationship is temporary, O lady. Your youthful body will be afflicted with old age and diseased one day and subsequently face death.

[Amba looks at both of them with surprise.]

Bimbisara :	Still, this body is man's all-in-all. Man enjoys everything through this and gratifies all his desires.
Buddha :	Is there any end to enjoyment? As *ghee*

		intensifies fire, desire in the human mind burns the body forever.
Bimbisara	:	What's the loss in that? Desire is the cause of all kinds of happiness.
Buddha	:	These are all your wrong perceptions. Desire is the cause of all kinds of sorrows. The end of desire leads to the end of sorrows.
Bimbisara	:	You do accept your life, Amba.
Buddha	:	You prepare yourself for *nirvana/moksha* (Salvation), *Devi*.

[Ambapali is confused here. She has to accept either social life or eternal life (salvation). Both the forms of Buddha and Bimbisara disappear.]

Last Scene

[It is Ambapali's Hall of Entertainment. Chapala comes running.]

Chapala	:	My noble lady! Where are you now?
Amba	:	(Hurriedly) What has happened? Has Tathagata reached? It's yet to be noon.
Chapala	:	Not Tathagata, but the King Bimbisara is coming.
Amba	:	King Bimbisara! At this time!
Chapala	:	The King is not alone…He is accompanied by a large procession of his army, chariots, elephants, and horses. In the middle of

		the procession, a bejewelled and gold-decked chariot run by six horses those are yoked together and surrounded by a well-arrayed army of Magadha. Nobody is sitting on the chariot. The King himself is coming riding on a white horse.
Amba	:	Then the King...? I have to accept either life or nirvana (salvation).

[Bimbisara enters and Chapala leaves.]

Bimbisara	:	Your bridegroom is present before you, my love. Why do you delay? Why do you hesitate? The entire state of Magadha is eagerly waiting for you to welcome. Do you know why? They want to know who that celestial unparalleled nymph is and for whom our Emperor himself is mad in love.
Amba	:	(Being astonished) Are you only mad after my beauty, *Maharaj*? The beauty of the body is transient and stays for a while and will lose its brightness...this curly black hair will whiten one day; this youth will experience its old age...then, your love for me will be diminished, won't it?
Bimbisara	:	(Smiling) Why are you talking incoherently today, my darling? Will the old age only come to you, but not to me? Will I be young throughout my entire life? The youth, old age and death are the rules of the life. Each one has to follow the rules. Why are you so worried about this?

Amba	:	Yes, Maharaj, each creature follows the rules. Can no one escape the cycles of birth and death? Can no one transcend this mundane firmament of sorrows and happiness, searching for eternal bliss?
Bimbisara	:	(Shocked) What has happened to you, my love!
Amba	:	I don't know what has happened to me. Since I don't know the answers, I am asking you the questions.
Chapala	:	(Entering) My lady! Tathagata has reached our principal entrance gate. For his reception,…
Amba	:	I am leaving now, Emperor…I am leaving now.
Bimbisara	:	(anxiously) Amba, my beloved!
Amba	:	Please, forgive me, O' King! Please forgive me. The answer to all my questions is standing at my door. For this auspicious moment, I have been waiting for ages for uncounted births. I leave now, Emperor.

[Ambapali walks with long steps. Chapala walks after her. The King of Magadha stands surprised.]

From the background of the stage is heard the chorus:
buddham śaranam gachchāmi.
sangham śaranam gachchāmi.
dharmam śaranam gachchāmi.

END

Black Eagle Books

www.blackeaglebooks.org
info@blackeaglebooks.org

Black Eagle Books, an independent publisher, was founded as a nonprofit organization in April, 2019. It is our mission to connect and engage the Indian diaspora and the world at large with the best of works of world literature published on a collaborative platform, with special emphasis on foregrounding Contemporary Classics and New Writing.

www.ingramcontent.com/pod-product-compliance
Lightning Source LLC
Chambersburg PA
CBHW060619080526
44585CB00013B/900